For the Empaths; those who feel what He felt.
Especially dedicated to
Cali, Emma and Kayla.

By Their
FRUIT

TULSA

ISBN: 978-1-957262-91-8
By Their Fruit

Yorkshire Publishing
1425 E 41st Pl
Tulsa, OK 74105
www.YorkshirePublishing.com
918.394.2665

Published in the USA

By Their
FRUIT

Poetry by
Matthew J Fratus

Preface

Is the Lord real to you? It's a question few of us ask ourselves. Many times, we're grandfathered into the faith of our families, parents, and friends. Practices are passed down, generation after genera-tion. Aspects of our inherited beliefs become thoughtless habits, (praying, saying "amen," or occasionally going to church). Many of us who partake in these habits often find ourselves uncomfort-able with the practicing habits of Christians who have, what they describe as an, "authentic relationship with God." It's an interest-ing concept, when the light of "belief" goes on, turning itself into an enduring faith that produces fruit. The Apostle Paul is one of the greatest example of this. As Saul of Tarsus, the "Pharisee of Pharisees," loved the law of God with such zeal, that he persecuted people he deemed a threat to it. Until his divine encounter with Jesus on the road to Damascus, it can be argued Paul, prayed fervently to the same God he was persecuting. God didn't have an authentic relationship with Saul of Tarsus, yet God saw the fruit Saul COULD grow, through the right circumstances.

So he emptied Saul to fill up Paul, giving new wine to pour out for all.

Paul would go forth and expand the gospel to the gentile nations beyond. He, a former persecutor of the church, stood now its greatest advocate, bearing good fruit wherever he was called. And with this incredible new calling came an authentic, imperishable relationship with God through faith in Jesus Christ and under the guidance of His divine Holy Spirit. The Lord became real to Paul. His prayers had new meaning. He saw the world completely different. Paul was ready to serve. Make no mistake, The Lord seeks the willing. He looks for the humble because only the humble can be like Christ. Christ was submissive, even onto death. He was a servant. Like Paul, the Lord knows how to prepare us for a servant's submission. He gave us a living depiction in Jesus and his everlasting gospel. A gospel that, like Paul's, begins in a wilderness state, under intense temptation and trial. So dear hurting friends, please know you're in divine company. We begin this way. It's not forever, but to prepare for the diamond to come, the coal must undergo a dramatic pressure. Before we can harvest, the ground must be made ready to produce. There's a reason for it. A new wineskin is being conceived. What was in the former, must first be spilled, poured out, and emptied. These poems reflect that very thing in my own life. I hope they bless you, as they did me. I hope you receive them in the knowledge that behind every line, every thought and note, is a sincerely flawed person; one broken by the same world you may be struggling to gain footing in. Take heart. Your new wine is coming. Let the old pour out of you, so that which you're being readied for, can flow beautifully inside. The choicest fruits are selected for the most cherished wine. Attached to the vine, we grow. When we are ripe, we can feed the world. The world will know us by our fruit.

Contents

Preface 7

Old to New: The Story of a Wineskin 11

    The Sentence 12
    End Thread 15
    The Restored Spirit 17
    The Intertwined Spirit 19
    The Spirit Uninhibited 21
    Speak for You 23
    The Wide and the Narrow 25

The Well from Which We Draw 27

    Gift of Salvation 28
    The Tested Spirit 30
    The Sermon 31
    Called 34
    I know You 37
    Right at the Door (Olivet) 40
    For You 42

Freely We Received; Freely We Give 45

The Readied Spirit 46
As You Are (at ease) 49
Well-Seasoned 51
The Redemptive Spirit 54
Life Is 57
The Spirit Unleashed 60
Commissioned 65

Old to New: The Story of a Wineskin

The Sentence

I knew a man
one time ago
this man did not know me.
His infamy
was all well-known,
his life was cold and bleak.

He saw the world
a certain way,
yet hated all he saw.
The joy of many,
those with plenty,
rubbed him chaffed and raw.

half his life
he held his hurt,
the other half
a grudge.
Until one day
this man
came face to face with a judge.

Guilty he was found.

Sentenced to death,
a just fate.
His crimes I am told
were too numerous to state.

Behind the walls, he waited
in agony and pain.
Counting down the few
tortured moments that remained.

As the seconds poured away
so, there could be no more,
the silence then was broken
by a jostle of the door.

He gently breathed his breath,
rose to his feet, and wiped his face.
Turned toward the guard
and put his head down in disgrace.

The guard escorted him
down the hall and through the door.
They came to the place
where this man's life would be no more.

As the man walked forward,
he was suddenly subdued.
The guard who walked beside him
softly whispered, "Me, not you."

The man stood confused,
a look of stupor crossed his face,

as he watched this guard
he never knew, take his place.

The guard turned and smiled,
before giving His last breath.
The man meanwhile
was pardoned
from a well-deserved death.

And to this day, I'm still amazed
He did what couldn't be.
That guard's name was "Jesus."
That former man was me.

End Thread

When I'm reliant on God, I don't resemble Him in those moments.
When I'm fully reliant on Him, I'm often tired, broken, or afraid.
I'm emotional, withdrawn, and unreasoning.

Unwilling to quit, but on the verge of surrender.
I begin to realize what I'm trying to carry simply cannot be carried
        by me.
And, for this, I'm angry.
I'm prideful.
I'm embarrassed to ask for what He's so eager to give.
Help. Love. Support.
Rest.

So, He allows me to tire myself, doing what my pride says I can.
It's in those exhaustive moments that I'm finally honest with Him.
Very honest.
Intent to be truthful and at my most sincere.
My heart, which He fully knows, aligns with the words in my prayers.
There's no caution thrown toward what I say or sound like.
It's here, at my most honest, that I am heard.
It's here that I, too, can hear Him.

I put down my burden with no choice but to let Him carry it.

Though my pride is heavy, what I've carried to this point is much
    heavier.
I watch Him load easily to himself what I couldn't continue with.
He wipes away my tears.
I enter His rest.
His beautiful rest.
In complete reliance of my God.

His rest then restores me.
With this beauty in hand, exchanged for my ashes, I become eager.
Eager to give of myself.
What has freely been given, I look freely to share.
When I rely on Him, the reliant becomes reliable once more.
The end of my rope is where His thread begins.

The Restored Spirit

A feeling stirs inside.
It is infrequent,
but present.
A warmth, or rather...
A sensation.

I feel it.
It calls to me.
Its voice; soft and sweet.
A melodious gentleness.
A whisper.

As that which comes "becomes,"
The presence becomes a bond.
What once was just a subtle stir,
Has grown into thoughts.

Two now think together,
where once, one stood alone.
Two minds and hearts
combining together.
Overlapping each other.
I feel Him.

Filling in the many gaps of my nature.
I'm becoming more.

The voice within corrects me.
He shares an opinion of all things.
Is it heavy? Weighted?
No.
It is gentle.
It is humble.
Yet, it is perfect.
I was once urgent to feel this.
Desperate to feel Him.
He is with me now.

The Intertwined Spirit

My life was once a certain way.
Though hard to recall, I can remember feelings; and that which I
    had to release.

Fear.
Fear was the time I gave to worry.
Fear was brought by overthought.
By wonder.
By trying to control that which cannot be.
Fear is unyielding.
It produces no fruit.
It bears no righteousness.
It has no place here.

Doubt.
Doubt was the time I gave to the thought of consequences.
Doubt was brought by confidence in the flesh.
By wondering, then wandering
By trying to control that which does not submit to me.
Doubt is unnerving.
It plunders my joy.
It hinders great people.
It has no place here.

Anxiousness.
Anxiousness is what becomes of fear and doubt.
The weed that culminates having grown unchecked.
Were I to pull the weed at fear,
Doubt would not exist.
Were I to pull the root up at doubt,
I would not find myself here.
Anxiousness is overwhelming.
It is subduing.
And yet, it is the first thing He takes on for me.
Because here, there is no room for it.

The Spirit Uninhibited

What is this destination?
This place?
The whisper has led me to this.
He's led me through this.
His voice; thunderous.
His guidance; gentle, yet decisive.
His intent; glorious.
I'm at His call.

Absent from that which hinders me.
Absent from that which binds.
Free from what used to control me.
Free to say "yes."
Free to say "no."
But led to say what is right.
He speaks for me today.
I hope to speak for Him tomorrow.
I'm at His call.

He reminds me of the many.
The brave who held to His voice.
Heroic in scripture;
yet humble in service.

Those whom I read of,
they now watch my chapters unfold.
We are connected.
Our mission is one.
Our mission is His.
I'm at His call.
He's readied me for His message.
I'm ready to speak for Him.

Speak for You

For as many years have been,
I know this much is true...
The faithful have received your word
so they could speak for you.

You do not call the proud,
they only see their point of view.
You carefully select
the humble heart that speaks for you.

You rarely call the rich,
they serve a God who isn't you.
You call those who endure,
and even more, they speak for you.

You will not call the sinful,
unless their hearts renew
and new wine is poured into them
so that they may speak for you.

You shall not call the lawless,
for the law comes from you.
A person absent from the law
is absent from the truth.

Gentle, full of mercy, seasoned with salt
to name a few.
Oh Lord, the traits you seek in saints
you call to speak for you.

So, Lord, may I endure the path
that's trodden on by few,
and receive the grace and boldness
so that I may speak for you.

The Wide and the Narrow

Happiness is of man;
joy is of God.

Happiness is pursued;
joy is given.

Happiness is weighted;
Joy is burdenless.

Happiness is temporal;
Joy is eternal.

Happiness is synthetic;
Joy is authentic.

Happiness is costly;
Joy is chargeless.

Happiness is of the flesh;
Joy is of the spirit.

Happiness is seasonal;
Joy is constant.

Happiness is blinding;
Joy is binding.

Happiness is popular;
Joy is prestigious.

Happiness needs a reason;
Joy surpasses all reason.

Happiness is of man;
Joy is of God.

The Well from Which We Draw

Gift of Salvation

Before He began, the Lord became man,
begotten and raised by His own.

Then came baptism. The spirit was given,
and wilderness became His home.

Many were called, though some were appalled
by this man from Galilee.

Many were healed by He who concealed
His true identity.

Soon was revealed His purpose.
Soon was revealed His end.

Soon was revealed His chosen,
who'd carry His words to Earth's ends.

After many miraculous things observed,
a darkness began to ignite.

And those who swore to uphold it,
turned against His heavenly light.

They lied and accused Him.
Struck and abused Him and judged perfection with sin.

Yet no matter the level of pain they inflicted
He prayed they'd be forgiven.

Whips were driven against His flesh,
flogged by the cat o' nine tails.

He was led to the place just beyond the gates
where they waited with three rusted nails.

So was fulfilled what the Prophets wrote.
It was finished with His last breath.

The guilty received their salvation,
while the innocent received His death.

The Tested Spirit

Is it love?
Does it feel like love?
Not the world's love,
His perfect love.
Is it patient?
Is it kind?
Does it boast?
Does it insist in itself?
In its own way or wisdom?
Is it irritable or resentful?
Is it steeped in truth or lies?
If it's love, it is Christ.
If it is Christ, it is found in His word.
If it's in His word, it's rested on my lips.
If it's on my lips, it is in my heart.
If it's in my heart, so is He.
If He's in my heart, I know love.
He is love.

The Sermon

Blessed are those whom the world despises,
blessed are those who mourn.
Blessed are those who are humble, meek,
those who seek Me in the storm.

Blessed are those persecuted for me,
those whom the world is against.
Blessed are you, the faithful and true,
who choose My recompense.

You are the salt of the earth, a light
that shines from the top of a hill.
You cannot be hidden the word that's been given
by the prophets has now been fulfilled.

Don't judge, but love.
Don't strike but be struck.
Endure all, and you will be mine.
Anger, lust, divorce, mistrust
must all be removed from your mind.

Give to the poor in secret.
Pray like I've taught you to do.

Lay up your treasure in Heaven.
Don't be anxious for clothes or food.

Ask, seek, and knock.
Treat others as if they were you.
Do not judge, or you will be judged,
a tree is known by its fruit.

Many will say they know me.
Many will say this indeed.
But many who do, I never knew
what awaits them is the gnashing of teeth.

For those who know me,
do as I do.
and what I do,
I do for Him.

By faith, you receive
the gift of grace.
By yourself
you only have sin.

Everyone then
who hears this
must make Me
the base of their lives.

Only my name
can withstand the rain,
when the
flooding waters, rise.

I am the rock and the cornerstone.
I'm the foundation for man.
Build with the tools I have given you,
and forever, your home shall stand.

Called

Today was a normal day.
I rose early to begin.
I ate breakfast with my wife.
I met my brother at my door.
We walked together to his yard.
We worked together to mend the rope.
We tied the knots tightly.
We carried the rope through the town.
We passed friends along the way.
Today was a normal day.

Today was another day.
We came to our destination.
Our friends had arrived before us.
They called out to us when they saw us.
We brought our ropes to the shore.
We stretched them out over the sand.
We baited our ropes and folded them.
We entered our small boat.
We pulled up the anchor.
We pushed out from the shore.
Today was another day.

Today was a long day.
We were patient.
Our ropes were well-baited.
The water was calm.
The breeze was cooled.
Hardly a motion to our boat.
Though peaceful, it's mostly unnoticed.
I'm fixated on my ropes.
We're fixated on them.
No matter where we drop them,
empty they are, when drawn in.
Hours and hours.

Today was a long day.

Today was a bad day.

I feel defeated.
Our nets have not netted.
Our catch; not caught.
Our investment; wasted.
My skin bears the soreness of too much sun.
My mind bears the weariness of too little faith.
Where was my God?
How often I prayed for help.
How often I called out.
"Help me, Lord."
"Help me catch something worthy!"
My only catch; silence.
Where is my God?
Today was a bad day.

Today, I am a failed fisherman
I am lost in the toil.
Lost in the understanding.
Our friends; equally dismayed.
So much time invested.
Nothing produced.
There's desperation here.
How will we eat?
How will I feed my family?
How can I face them?
How can I return to them with these nets?
These filthy, emptied nets.
Does God even see this?
It seems a crowd has gathered nearby.
Spectators, to revel in my failures.
They see this, I'm sure.
They're being taught by someone.
He sees this, too, my embarrassment.
Why does He suddenly stare at me?
Why does His gaze look to mine?
Why is He leaving His Group?
Why is He walking towards me?
To revel in my pain and failure, most likely.
What could He possibly want from me?
Me; a fisherman.
Me, with nothing to show for myself.
No fish.
No catch.
Just wet,
empty nets.
What could this man want with me?

I know You

I am fully known to You?
Did you know Cain would kill as Abel prayed to you?
Did Noah know how to swim?
Why did Job suffer over a bet?
Were you aware of the doubts in Sarah's heart?
Did Abraham feel confliction with Isaac?
Why did you put up with so much from Jacob?
Why did your people experience Egypt if you love them?
Why couldn't you forgive Moses and let him see the land?
Why was King Saul chosen by you?
Why did you put up with David?
Why does Solomon's end seem so tragic?
Why did Elisha have the bear do that to children?
Why did Isaiah suffer such a death?
Why did you allow Babylon?
What did Jeremiah, Ezekiel, and Daniel do to receive your favor?
Why were you so quiet before the coming?

You are.
I did. And I was with Abel when it happened.
Noah's swimming prowess wasn't a qualification.
To show my most disobedient child he was wrong.
I was.

Painfully, yes.
I knew what Jacob would become.
They are my children, and I knew THEIR hearts.
He is my son, and his place was with me.
Israel needed to experience him to appreciate David.
David is my son, and I know his heart.
To teach others an important lesson.
Elisha did not, it was me, and I knew their hearts.
Because he was willing.
Because Israel was unwilling.
They were willing.
I was saving my word for that moment.

Am I fully saved by grace?
What about the time I really messed up?
The one time I did what nobody knows?
Has anyone sinned as great as I've sinned?
Has anyone failed as much as I've failed?
How do I know that your word is the truth?
Why is it so hard to follow you?
Why are there so many hardships?
Why is their suffering and pain?
Why don't you end it for the sake of your elect?
Why do we need to continue?
Why are you tolerating this world?
Why are we becoming so evil?
Why is everything getting worse?
Why is faith hard to hold onto?
Why is sin so easy for me?
Why do you love me?
How much, Lord?

You are.
Forgiven.
Say it aloud, forgiven.
All will fall short.
Falling short is a constant.
Have faith in my word, and it will convict you.
Because the evil one doesn't want you to find me.
Because the evil one hates that I've found you.
Where do you turn in these moments?
Would you leave your children behind somewhere if all weren't collected?
For the sake of the lost, I am calling to Me.
Because of how much I love those still in it.
The evolution of sin.
Hearts are becoming harder.
Because it is precious.
Because you are precious, and your enemy knows it.
Because I know you.
Fully, my child.

Right at the Door
(Olivet)

They will come in My name
leading many astray,
starting wars and rumors of war.
See to it you are not alarmed, my child,
for your Lord is right at the door.

Nation will rise against nation.
Famines and earthquakes will try to implore.
They're just the beginning
of birth pains from sinning.
The Lord is still right at the door.

Captured, arrested, put to death,
tested, a hatred my saints will endure.
They'll betray many lives,
false prophets will rise,
yet the Lord is right at the door.

Lawlessness will increase.
The love of most will grow cold and impure.
Yet the gospel will span,

over every land,
as your Lord stands right at the door.

This is a call for the strength
and perseverance for what you'll endure.
Tribulation will come,
but so shall the Son
who is standing right at the door.

For You

I did these things for you.
I hope you know that's true.
I took your place
and gave you grace.
My child, this was for you.

I took these blows for you.
I knew what they would do.
When I declared
that God prepared
a King for the Jews.

I included you.
The Gentiles and the Jews.
All are invited,
though some will deny it.
But all were welcomed in truth.

I took judgement for you.
Their judgement I already knew.
They laughed and lavished,
released Barabbas,
yet I could only think of you.

I took those whips for you.
Do you know what those whips can do?
They tear your flesh,
add labor to breath,
yet I happily took them for you.

I carried my cross for you.
It was something I had to do.
When the weight was too much,
Simon showed up,
And we carried my cross for you.

Those nails were meant for you.
But my child, I refuse,
for you to receive
what they did to me,
with the nails that were meant for you.

This cross I'm against is for you.
I did what I came to do.
And, as my breath labors
I've shown you my favor.
On this cross that was built for you.

I gave up my life for you.
You'll never feel what was due.
Though life will bring trials,
there should be no denial.
What's owed to you won't reach you.

They buried my body for you.
In a cold and lonely tomb.

In burial clothes,
yet the third day, I rose
to prepare a place with many rooms.

I told them to find you.
Those that received the truth.
Therefore their mission
The great commission
Is to go out and teach it to you.

I'm coming back for you.
I promised my church in truth.
Let there be no doubt
when my church hears the shout,
The Lord has returned for you.

Freely We Received; Freely We Give

The Readied Spirit

We draw from that we know is true.
We pray for wisdom through and through.
We bring ourselves to the cross.
Our life begins where His was lost.
We ask forgiveness in His name.
We then forgive how He forgave.
We bring with us all that we know,
to the places that we go.
The Readied Spirit is with us.

We carry that which we hold dear.
We know our savior's always near.
I hear His voice inside my heart.
We now shall never be apart.
Connected by His saving grace.
His spirit goes to every place.
I am the temple; now they'll see
His spirit goes with me.
The Readied Spirit goes with us.

Do they see the spirit within me?
In my sermons, when I speak?
Do they hear the voice I hear?

If so, why do they carry fear?
Why do they worry, doubt and hate?
Why do they judge each other's plate?
Why can't they see what you've shown me?
Oh spirit, let them see.
The Readied Spirit speaks to us.

Not all will hear, nor all believe.
But many will receive the seed.
One day it will grow by faith
and those who hold it will be saved.
Soon they will produce a crop.
This rescue mission doesn't stop.
Until you hear the trumpet shout,
your Lord is what your life's about.
The Readied Spirit teaches us.

You may tire or feel fatigue.
You may be called into disease.
You might feel loss that some won't know.
All this is placed to help you grow.
No matter what you feel or say,
Your Lord forgives each end of day.
So give to all what you've received
and when you speak, I'll speak.
The Readied Spirit speaks for us.

When you fall, and you WILL fall
The Lord will come to rescue all.
You do not have to live afraid
The Lord will never be away.
You may not always feel His peace.

Your enemy prowls like a beast.

And wants you well beyond His grace,
but you are His forever place.
The Readied Spirit fights for us.

Upon His death, the temple curtain tore for all to see.
I am His temple; where I go, my Lord now goes with me.
The Readied Spirit <u>Leads us</u>.

As You Are (at ease)

You will stumble, fall, and fail.
At ease.
You will cry, scream, and wail.
At ease.
You'll endure many trials,
because you're My child,
but through it all be...
At ease.

Find a degree of peace.
Then let that peace never cease.
Stay in my word
and recount all you've heard.
But, in all, you do be...
At ease.

They should consider you least.
But the least is first at My feast.
So serve others first
and quench others' thirst.
While you work, please be...
At ease.

At ease, my child, at ease.
This is not a place easy to be.
But the spirit inside you
will never deride you.
Abide in Him and be...
At ease.

You may try to be more than you should.
A road that leads nowhere good.
Your part in the story
is showing My glory.
For you couldn't do what I could.

All are saved by grace.
All will see My face.
Let every knee bow
and confess all aloud.
For the lamb that was slain in their place.

So at ease my child until.
My spirit shows you my will.
I won't leave or forsake you,
so be how I made you.
Be at ease.
Peace be still.

Well-Seasoned

What part of love is anger?
What part of love is rage?
What part of love does hate come from?
Why can't we turn this page?

Why do we judge our brothers
and our sisters like we do,
when all we're ever called to judge
is trees producing fruit?

Why do we lean on knowledge
when His wisdom's given free?
How can we think our condescension
shows our deep belief?

How can we do the work of Christ
and not be who He was?
How can we think we're doing right
by never showing love?

How can we claim that love is
only shown through our rebuke?
How can we offer our world something

Jesus didn't do?

How can we pretend love
is not defined in what we know?
How can we ignore Paul
and the letters that he wrote?

If we fail at one thing,
we've surely failed at all.
Fortunately, grace is there
to save us when we fall.

But showing something other
than the savior that we know,
is not a path you'll find
on our long and narrow road.

And being something less
is also something that's forbidden.
We must produce a crop
with the talents we are given.

So to believers everywhere,
commissioned by the Lord...
Show what you've been shown.
Show no less and show no more.

For you've received a savior;
an example of perfection.
You now owe the world more
than your self-righteous correction.

You've received His grace, my friend,
not by what you've earned.
So be a better student
and show others what you've learned.

The Redemptive Spirit

I've fallen.
I've failed.
My goal.
Unprevailed.
My efforts,
in vain
it would seem.

I was called.
I was blessed.
I was challenged.
Many tests.
Now this pain.
Please, please,
intervene.

I have suffered
many things.
I hear no
angel wings.
Are you with me?
As I suffer and I bleed?

These steps,
they were ordered
by the Lord.
Why did I falter?
Why did I
not receive
what I would need?

I have fallen.
I have failed.
How can the Lord
not prevail?
How can the Lord
in all His wisdom
forgive me?

When All
that I read
of those
who served
His every need
is how successful
all they did
turned out
to be.

And here
I now stand.
A failure's stare,
and empty hands.
Broken plans
that have reduced me

to my knees.
But it's here,
a gentle voice
lifts me with
a gentle hoist
and says,
"You're absolutely
Where you're supposed to be."

Life Is

Before we are formed
He knows us.
Before we draw breath
we are His.

Each one is made wonderfully
in His sight.
The presence of life
is a gift.

It's not one
that's given to all.
Though to all,
it is preciously held.

Not just the
life in the womb,
but the life
that you hold to yourself.

A decision was made
to bring you
from the womb,

to give life
to your body and soul.

And no matter the weight
or the hardship it made,
your life was
a sight to behold.

So who can be given
their life as a gift
and choose otherwise for the unborn?

Who can receive the air that they breathe
and believe in the need for scorn?

Yet, who can be clear,
in the presence of fear
and the choices
it helps us to make?

How can we judge
the person God loves,
regardless of
such a mistake?

For without the Lord
and His council,
we might all be
swayed by the herd.

And the sorrow
that comes

after it's done,
can only be healed by His word.

So to anyone bearing
the weight of a choice;
a decision they
now never meant...

All have sinned;
all fallen short
and the Lord forgives
all who repent.

The Spirit Unleashed

A seed.
Beware the mustard seed.
You've been warned.
Beware that subtle whisper.
Beware the call that ushers forth.
While yearning to know it
You might be swept up.
Gathered onto it.
Caught in its web.
It is ceaseless.
Enduring.
And many have bled.
Many have shed more
than blood or sweat.
They've shed the weakness of their skin.
Of their former flesh.
Of their former self.
Their gold and their wealth.
Their namesakes and purpose.
That once was divine.
Once was unblemished.
Hidden in comfort.
Lost in a lifestyle.

Among the thorns,
Though once adorned.
This wide road they were on.
And now to it,
they cannot return.
Beware that pesky seed
For which the saints yearn.

That seed.
It is small.
Smaller than most.
Small in size and impression.
Once fallen, it's unfinding.
Once hidden, it's lost.
Washed by the drizzle,
Lost in the frost.
A seed simply gone.
Too delicate for some.
Too minuscule to the eye.
Infinitesimal.
A fraction of a decimal.
Unimpressive in stature.
Uneeded as sustenance.
Useless to most.
When seen, it's forgotten.
Not precious,
nor something we seek.
What can a seed
with such a small stature
bring to a world
With so much disaster?
Who has a need

For that seed?

A tree.
A yellow tree.
A yellow tree for all to see.
Though small as small
Could possibly be,
That needless seed
Is now a tree.
With years behind it
Sun to guide it
and rain to water its roots,
that seed that exceeded
no seed it preceded,
has now become something anew.
Protection for those
who find Him.
Like birds that now
perch on its branch.
Kept from the heat
that would harm them.
By the gold
That it holds
In its hands.
A tree.
This seed.
It became a tree.
Tall and long
For all to see.
Though many fools
were fools like me,
I'll gladly rest

beneath this tree.

That tree.
That beautiful golden tree.
It's grown some more
since last I'd seen.
It's taller than
all other trees.
How precious is
that tree indeed.
I see.
I see
this beautiful tree.
At first,
the worst
assumed by me
was aimed at that
unimpressive seed.
Of which
Bore forth this tree.
Indeed.
A fool
indeed is me.
For I prejudged
that little seed
and wrote it off
as just a weed.
No greater a fool
can be than me.
And so henceforth
I say, indeed,
About from which

Came from that seed.
A mighty
and impressive tree,
that for my life
Will shelter me.

Commissioned

Let's speak honestly.
Truthfully.
Needful and robust.
Approachable, quotable.
Graceful and just.
Let's give Him time
and our every thought.
Let our wording be
always wrought,
with righteousness
that was bought,
from Him in which
all things are taught.
Be clear.
Be present.
Be Him,
Authentic!
Not for the cheers
of the present crowd,
for cheers from those
beyond the clouds.
Be courageous.
True.

Convicted.
Be you!
Selected to do
what he's called you
To do.
Speak to them.
Speak for him.
Be willing
to ignore them.
Plead with them.
Lead them.
Love them.
Implore them.
The darkness covering
through the night
has nothing on
the coming light.
A dawn will shine
and all that's bright
will break the dark
in a show of might.
We shall be patient
And endure.
We know the king
we're fighting for.
We know that king
Has bled for us
and now awaits
the rest of us
to turn to Him
and see his face.
Forgiven of sin.

Receiving grace.
And not a soul
will be lost.
He's paid the price.
We've counted the cost.
And all we've done.

All we've become.
All we gave up at the cross.
It's tossed aside
by Christ,
replaced with life
that can't be lost.
Glorious!
Glory!
Hallelujah!
Mercy!
His name be praised all days!
Until our Lord returns
we must demonstrate
His ways.
Spread the news of grace.
The tomb an empty grave.
The urgency of faith.
The narrow path that isn't paved.
The price our savior paid.
The sin that He forgave.
A great falling away
will precede his coming day.
Be strong.
Courageous.
Infectious.

Contagious.
Not loud
or audacious.
Be great.
He was.
Be present
He is.
Be all the world
can never give.
Be love.
The deepest
most important rule
our Lord said
should be felt...
Love the Lord
your God
and love others
as yourself.
Many forgo
those words.
They think only
with their head.
But a ministry without love
is a ministry that's dead.
The heart is so important.
Guard it! Protect it!
The world
won't respect it.
They choose
to reject it.
Their faith
is neglected.

Unwatered,
sedentary.
Either Asleep
or in a hurry.
No time for the weary
or the message that we carry.
They've found their
lives to live.
I've found there's
more to give.
There's more sand
here to sift
and what's good
may be buried.
What's God
can't be hurried.
And what's hidden
is a gift.
His word reveals his word.
So as you read,
what you read,
remember
what you've heard.
He was bold for you.
Be bold with the truth.
You will be hated
for what's stated.
Be patient.
He was with you.
The word.
The word.
Stay in the word!

The word is the
essence of faith.
No matter how much
you can quote it
for others,
applying the word
is what saves.

Time, time.
Time is short.
Shorter with each day.
The Lord will
soon return
and take
the faithful ones
away.

Away they go.
In the clouds.
To their
eternal home.
I Hope
the Lord returns
at the conclusion
of this poem.

(If so, see you there!)

CPSIA information can be obtained
at www.ICGtesting.com
Printed in the USA
JSHW040042200723
45076JS00009B/165